# A Midnight Wrestling Match

**Genesis:** *Chapters 31:3—33:4*

Issac had twin sons Esau and Jacob. Before their birth, God told Rebekah, their mother that unlike the practice of the day when the elder son became the head of the family, her younger son would become the head of the family.

Now, Rebekah loved her younger son Jacob more than Esau. Esau was more interested in outdoor activities while Jacob remained indoors mostly. One day, when Issac was about to give his special blessings to his first born Esau, by a trick Rebekah extracted his blessings for Jacob. As Issac was old and partially blind, he could not differentiate between his two sons.

After Esau found that he had lost his birthright and his father's blessings, he was very angry with his brother Jacob. He said to himself, and told others, 'My father Isaac is very old and won't live long. As soon as he dies, I shall kill Jacob for having robbed me of my birthright!'

When Rebekah heard this, she said to Jacob, ‘Before it is too late, go away from home and get out of Esau’s sight. Perhaps when Esau sees you no longer, he will forget his anger. And then, you can come home again. Go and visit my brother Laban, your uncle in Haran, and stay with him for a little while.’

Jacob stayed for a long time in the land of Haran, much longer than he had thought of staying. And with time he became rich. Jacob took a share of the sheep, oxen and camels as wages for his work from his Uncle Laban. And as Jacob was very wise and careful at his work, his share of cattle and flock grew larger. After twenty years, Jacob decided to go back to the land of Canaan, to his Father Isaac, who was still living, though was very old.

Jacob did not tell his Uncle Laban that he had decided to go away. One day while Laban was away from home, Jacob gathered together his wives and children and all his sheep, cattle and camels, and went away quietly.

When Laban found that Jacob had left him, he was very displeased because Jacob managed his cattle better than him. And moreover, God blessed everything that Jacob undertook. Laban also did not like to have his two daughters, the wives of Jacob, taken away from him. So Laban and the men followed Jacob. That night, God spoke to Laban in a dream and said, 'Do not harm Jacob when you meet him.'

And so, when Laban came to where Jacob had put up his camp on Mount Gilead on the east of the River Jordan, he spoke kindly to Jacob. They piled up a heap of stones, and on it they set up a large rock like a pillar. As they sat beside the heap of stones and ate a meal together, they made a promise. They promised not to harm each other, ever.
And then Laban kissed his daughters, Jacob's two wives, and all of Jacob's children, and bade them good bye. After this incident, Laban went back to Haran and Jacob went to Canaan.

When Jacob was going back to Canaan, he heard that Esau, his brother, was coming to meet him with an army of four hundred men. He knew how angry Esau had been long before, and how he had threatened to kill him. He feared that Esau would not only kill him but his wives and his children too. If Jacob had acted rightly toward his brother, he need not have feared Esau's coming.

That night Jacob divided his family and belongings into two parts so that if one part was attacked, the other part might escape. And he sent a great flock of oxen, cows, sheep, goats, camels and asses for his brother hoping that he would be kind towards him. And then Jacob prayed

earnestly to the Lord God to help him. After that, he sent all his family across a brook while he stayed alone on the other side of the brook to pray.

When Jacob was alone, he felt that a man had taken hold of him, and Jacob wrestled with this strange man all night. The man was an angel from God. They wrestled so hard that Jacob's thigh was strained. At dawn the angel said, 'Let me go, for the day is breaking.'

But Jacob said, 'I will not let you go until you bless me!' At this, the angel said, 'From now your name shall be 'Israel', meaning *one who wrestles with God*, for you have wrestled with God and have won victory.'

When the sun rose and the angel had left him, Jacob gave a name to that place where he was. He called it *Peniel* or *Penuel*, which in the language that Jacob spoke, meant *The Face of God*. And after this Jacob was lame, for while wrestling he had strained his thigh.

Early next morning, Esau came to meet Jacob and they met face to face!

Jacob bowed to Esau over and over again, as people do in those lands when they meet someone of a higher rank. But Esau ran and placed his arms around his neck and kissed him. The two brothers wept together. Esau was kind and generous and forgave his brother for all the wrong that he had done. He also accepted all the gifts that Jacob had brought for him. And so the quarrel was ended and the two brothers were at peace.

After this, Jacob went to Shechem, a place lying in the middle of Canaan and set up his tents there. Although, there were streams of water all around, he dug his own well. This is the same well where Jesus sat and talked with a woman many ages after that time.

As Jacob was also called Israel, all his descendants were called Israelites.

Meanwhile, Esau with his children and his cattle went away to a land in the southeast of Canaan, called Edom.

And Jacob and his family lived in the land of Canaan dwelling in tents and moving from place to place, where they could find good pasture to feed their flocks.